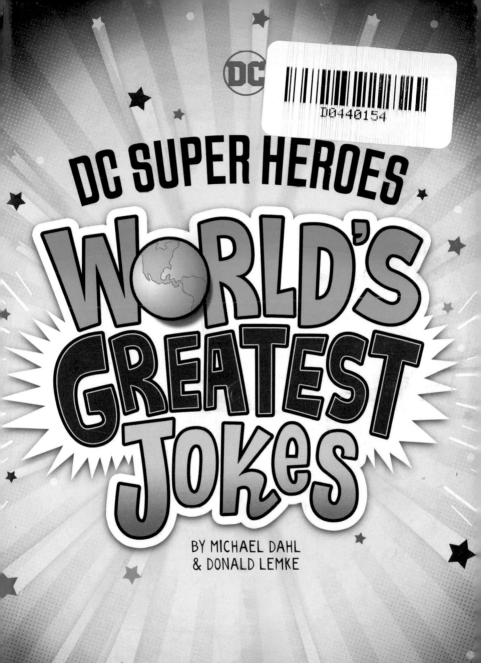

DC SUPER HEROES

WORLD'S GREATEST JOKES

BY MICHAEL DAHL
& DONALD LEMKE

Capstone Young Readers
a capstone imprint

Published by Capstone Young Readers in 2018
A Capstone Imprint
1710 Roe Crest Drive
North Mankato, Minnesota 56003
www.capstonepub.com

STAR39765

Cataloging-in-Publication Data is available on the
Library of Congress website.

ISBN: 978-1-68436-002-4 (paperback)
ISBN: 978-1-68436-003-1 (eBook)

Summary: With hundreds of kid-approved jokes
and full-color artwork, this official DC Comics joke book will have
readers — KA-BOOM! — exploding with laughter!

Designer: Brann Garvey

Printed in China.
001482

CONTENTS

CHAPTER ONE

MONSTER JOKES!

Why did Aquaman sleep with a night-light?
He was afraid of sea monsters under his bed!

What is the scariest place for Aquaman to swim?
Lake Eerie.

What is the second scariest place for Aquaman to swim?
The Dead Sea.

What did Aqualad say when he
first saw an ocean monster?

"See? Serpent!"

What is Aquaman's secret weapon
for defeating sea monsters?

His mussels.

What is a
sea monster's
favorite dish?

**Fish and
ships!**

What did Lex Luthor get when he crossed a skunk with a giant?

A big stink!

What happened when a monster
ate Lex Luthor's uranium?
He got atomic-ache!

What did Lex Luthor get when he crossed
Comet the Super-Horse with a monster?
A night-mare.

What did Lex Luthor create when
he combined a cocker spaniel,
a poodle, and a ghost?
A cocker-poodle-boo!

I have a
hair-raising
story about
a monster . . .

Well,
don't tell
Lex Luthor!

What do you call Krypto the Super-Dog when he sees a monster?

Super Pet-rified!

Why did Krypto and the werewolf stop fighting?

They were both dog-tired.

How did Krypto lose track of the evil monster?

He was barking up the wrong tree!

What type of Super-Pet is good at catching vampires?

A blood hound.

What do you get when you cross
Supergirl with a ghost?
Super-ghoul!

What did Jimmy Olsen get
when he took a photo of a
two-headed monster?
A double exposure!

What happens when a monster rides in Wonder Woman's Invisible Jet?

It's a terror-flying experience!

Where do cyclops come from?
Paradise Eye-land.

What is as tall as Giganta but doesn't weigh anything?

Giganta's shadow!

How can you tell when Green Arrow
is afraid of monsters?

He has a quiver.

Is the Atom ever afraid
of monsters?

Just a tiny bit!

What does Silver Banshee
put on her bagels?

Scream cheese.

What is Silver Banshee's favorite
ice cream topping?

Whipped scream!

What do you call a
Bizarro mummy?
Daddy.

What do you call a
Bizarro vampire?
Alive.

What do you call a
Bizarro werewolf?
A therewolf.

What do you call a Bizarro insect?
An outsect.

Why did Lois Lane choose to write her news story at a cemetery?

Because there are so many plots there!

What happened when the ghost
visited the Daily Planet Building?

**He turned
Perry White!**

What is General Zod's
favorite musical?

**Phantom Zone
of the Opera.**

What did Bizarro say to his son after
he hadn't seen him for a while?

You grew-some.

Where did zombie
Bizarro come from?

Crypt-on!

How does Superman keep
zombies from invading the
Fortress of Solitude?

He uses a
dead-bolt lock!

Has Wonder Woman ever seen
the Abominable Snowman?
Not Yeti!

What side of Titano has
the most hair?
The outside.

Why can't the cyclops see anymore?
**Wonder Woman
caught his eye.**

What does Titano call an
exploding monkey?
A ba-boom!

What happens when
Batman gets scared?
**He gets
Bruce-bumps.**

What happened when
the Joker saw a ghost?
He got scared silly!

What road in Gotham City has the
most ghosts haunting it?
A dead end.

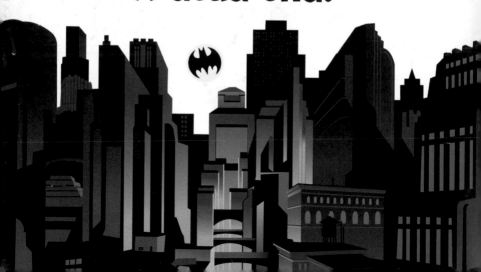

Why does the Joker sleep with the lights on?
Because he's afraid of the Dark Knight!

What did Mr. Freeze say when he saw the Abominable Snowman? **"Icy you!"**

What's the difference between Batman and the Abominable Snowman?

One likes justice, and the other likes just ice.

What do you get if a huge, hairy monster steps on Batman and Robin?

Flatman and Ribbon!

Why did Dracula visit the Batcave?

To hang out!

Where does zombie Batman like to hide?

The Bat-grave.

What do you get
when you cross
The Flash with
a monster?

**Scary
Allen!**

What kind of fur can you
get from Gorilla Grodd?

**As fur away
as possible!**

Which hand should you
use to pet Titano?

Someone else's!

What did Superman say to the giant
ape when it did something wrong?

"Titano-no!"

What does Titano call a
well-balanced meal?

**A hero in
each hand!**

What do you get when you cross
Hal Jordan with a ghost?
Scream Lantern!

What do you get when you cross Hal
Jordan with the Abominable Snowman?
Mean Lantern!

How are Sinestro and
a scaredy-cat alike?

They're both yellow.

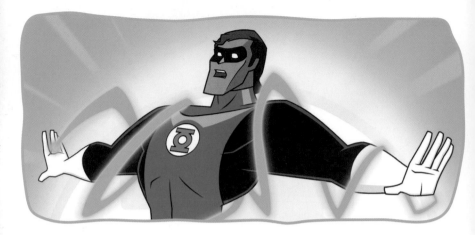

What's the safest way to explore a dark, scary cave?

Take a Lantern with you!

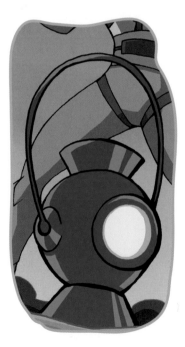

What does Glomulus want
to be for Halloween?
A goblin!

How did Zatanna make
the Minotaur fall asleep?
**She turned him into
a bull-dozer!**

What would you call 144
Swamp Things stuffed in a box?
Gross.

How does Scarecrow keep
cool in the summer?
**He uses a
scare-conditioner!**

WHY DIDN'T GRODD EAT THE FLASH?

He hated fast food!

Why did Shazam suspect his
father was a vampire?

Because he's
a Bat-son!

What did The Flash find between
the giant monster's toes?

Slow runners!

What type of truck does
Gorilla Grodd drive?
A monster truck!

What do you call Gorilla Grodd
in a phone booth?
Stuck.

When is a wall like Killer Croc?
When it is scaled.

How does the villain
Scarecrow like his eggs?
Terror-fried!

What's the swamp-dwelling villain
Solomon Grundy's favorite snack?
Marsh-mallows!

What happens when Nightwing sees a zombie?
He gets flight-ened!

Why shouldn't villains
make Batman angry?

**He's got a very
bat temper!**

Why is Killer Croc so good at creeping up on people?
He's a crept-tile.

What did Scarecrow wear to the fancy dinner?
A boo-tie!

Why don't Batman or Dracula have many friends?
They both have bat-breath.

What do the Joker and Dr. Frankenstein have in common?

They both keep you in stitches!

What is Scarecrow's favorite fruit?
Straw-berries.

What do little monsters like
to ride at the amusement park?
The scary-go-round.

What is Scarecrow's favorite color?
Blooooo!

Why does Scarecrow have
good hearing?
**Because he's
so ear-ie.**

Where did baby Scarecrow go
while his parents were at work?
Day-scare!

What does Scarecrow like to eat for supper?
Spook-etti!

DAILY PLANET DEADLINES!

SUPERMAN BATTLES THE LOCH NESS MONSTER

by Scott Land

CYBORG'S ATTACK

by Ann Droid

BIZARRO EXILED FROM EARTH

by Nada Lowd

KILLER CROC ON THE LOOSE!

by Ali Gader

TITANO CLIMBS DAILY PLANET BUILDING!

By Andover Hand

WHO'S ROBBING GRAVES IN GOTHAM CITY?

by Ivan Alibi

DRACULA STEALS BATMOBILE!

by Grant Otto Theff

BATMAN TURNS INTO WEREWOLF

by Oliver Sudden

What do you call Solomon Grundy
when he uses a phone?
A dead ringer!

Which of Superman's foes is
the easiest to defeat?
Lex Loser!

How is Wonder Woman's
Invisible Jet like a blizzard?
When you look outside, there's sno-wing in sight!

Where is the Gotham City
cemetery located?
In the dead center of town.

How did the hairdresser beat
The Flash in a race?

She knew a shortcut!

What's black and white
and red all over?

The Penguin with
a sunburn!

What happened when Wonder
Woman trapped Cheetah
with her lasso?

The villain
was knot
happy!

WHICH WEAPON OF WONDER WOMAN'S DIDN'T DO A VERY GOOD JOB?

Her lasso-so.

1. What time is it when you see a monster?

2. What room is useless for a ghost?

3. Where does Dracula keep his money?

4. How do you make a witch itch?

5. Why do werewolves have such large families?

6. What do ghosts like for dessert?

ANSWERS:

1. Time to run.
2. A living room.
3. A blood bank.
4. Take away the W.
5. Each has four paws.
6. Ice cream.

CHAPTER TWO

ANIMAL JOKES!

Why does Supergirl's cat, Streaky,
keep running in circles?

**Do you know
how hard it is to
run in squares?**

Why did Wonder Woman's pet,
Jumpa, go to the hospital?

**She needed a
hop-eration!**

How did the octopus
make Aquaman laugh?

With ten-tickles!

Why did Bumblebee have sticky hair?

**Because she uses
a honey-comb!**

How did Krypto get away
from Lex Luthor?

He made his S-cape.

Why did Batman
arrest the sheep?

**It made
an illegal
ewe-turn!**

Did you hear the joke about the skunk
trapped in the Batmobile?
Never mind. It stinks!

What did Robin say when Catwoman
escaped from Arkham Asylum?
"It's a cat-astrophe!"

What did Robin get
when he trained with
a pig karate master?
**Pork
chops!**

When is the Joker like a pony?
When he's a little hoarse!

Who's the green super hero bovine
who comes from another planet?
The Martian Moo-hunter!

What do you call a
Bizarro flamingo?
A flamin-stop.

What do you call a Bizarro buffalo?
A buffa-high.

What do you get when you cross Cyborg with a pig?
A Cy-boar!

What do Green Arrow and a herd of
cattle have in common?
Bull's-eyes.

Why did Killer Croc go to jail?
Because he's a crook-odile!

Which are the brightest pets
in Aquaman's kingdom?

The rays.

Do they serve crabs at
Aquaman's new restaurant?

**They serve
everybody.
Have a seat!**

What did Aquaman do when
he saw the blue whale?

**Tried to cheer
it up!**

Where does Comet the
Super-Horse live?

In a neigh-borhood!

Why did Jumpa look so sad?
She was a little un-hoppy.

When does Comet the Super-Horse talk?
Whinny wants to!

Why can't Cheetah hide from Wonder Woman?
Because she's always spotted.

What happened when Cheetah stood behind Jumpa?
She got a real kick out of it!

Why doesn't Wonder Woman's worst enemy fight fair?
Because she's a Cheetah!

What do Cheetah and
The Flash have in common?
**They both like
fast food!**

What is Catwoman's favorite color?
Purr-ple.

Where is Catwoman's favorite
place to vacation?
Purrrr-u.

What happened when
a lion ate the Joker?
He felt funny!

Where should Streaky go if
he loses his tail?
A re-tail store.

What happened when Ace the
Bat-Hound swallowed a watch?
**He got a lot
of ticks!**

Why is Streaky the Super-Cat
a good crime fighter?
He can smell a rat.

DID YOU KNOW KRYPTO LIKES TO SMELL FLOWERS?

He's a bud hound!

What's Krypto's favorite dessert?
Pup-cakes!

Batman: "Where do fleas go in winter?"
Ace the Bat-Hound: "Search me!"

How is Ace the Bat-Hound like a smartphone?
They both have collar I.D.!

Why doesn't Superman let Krypto ever use his DVD player?
Because he always hits paws.

Where do Krypto, Ace the Bat-Hound,
and Streaky like to vacation?

The city of Pet-ropolis!

What do you call a baby kanga that
always stays indoors?

A pouch potato.

How did Batman stop Ace the
Bat-Hound from barking inside
the Batcave?

He put him outside.

Why does Batman bring his pet
when he chases after his enemy?

**Because Ace always
beats a Joker.**

When does Batman take
Ace for a walk?

**When it's time to
do his duty!**

What is Beppo the Super-Monkey's
favorite snack?

**Chocolate chimp
cookies!**

How does Batman stay so clean?
He takes a lot of bats!

What did Comet the Super-Horse say when he tripped?
I fell down, and I can't giddy-up!

What's Hawkwoman's favorite dessert?
Magpie!

Where did Superman find the missing lion?
On Mane Street!

Why can birds see Wonder Woman's Invisible Jet?

Because it's in di-skies!

Why did Hawkman and Hawkwoman
fly south for the winter?

**Because it was
too far to walk.**

What did Hawkwoman say
when she was cold?

Brrrrrrrrrrd!

Why couldn't the Penguin pay
for dinner at the restaurant?

**His bill was
too big!**

Why didn't the octopus join
the Justice League?

**He was more suited
for the arm-y.**

What do you get when you cross
a waterfowl with Batman?
Goose Wayne!

What did Robin say when he saw
a low-flying bird?
"Duck!"

Which of Penguin's dirty birds
liked stealing things?
The robber ducky.

How many skunks could
fit in the Batmobile?
Quite a phew!

Why is Robin always so happy?
Because he's not a blue bird.

What do you get when you
cross Superman's girlfriend with
a bird that has long legs?
Lois Crane!

How does Shazam's Super-Pet,
Hoppy, go on vacation?
By Hare-plane.

How did the Penguin fly
south for the winter?
In his private jet.

Who's the green super hero duck
that comes from another planet?
Marshy Manhunter!

Why didn't the police
believe Cheetah?

They thought
she was a lion!

WHY WAS THE PENGUIN THROWN OFF THE BASEBALL TEAM?

He could only hit fowl balls!

Why are porcupines Green Arrow's
favorite animals?

**Because they have
a lot of quills.**

Why did the lemur have
rings on its tail?

**It hoped to become
a Green Lantern!**

Where did the two Amazon
rodents come from?
Pair-O-Mice Island!

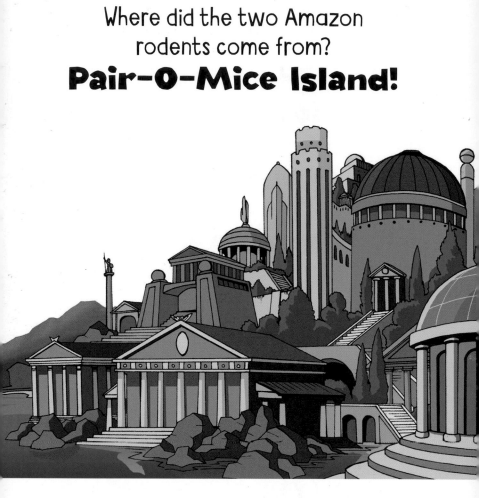

What kind of book does Wonder
Woman's kanga like to read?
One with a hoppy
ending!

Why did Wonder Woman take her kanga to the hospital?

She needed a hop-eration.

What happened when Superman skipped college and flew to the Sun?

He got a million degrees!

How does Green Lantern spend his time in art class?

Color-ring.

When Solomon Grundy was young there were only 25 letters in the alphabet.

Nobody new why.

Why is Ace the Bat-Hound always on time?

He's a great watch dog!

What is Titano's favorite month?
Ape-ril!

Why did Titano climb up the
side of the building?
The elevator
was broken!

Why does Beppo the Super-Monkey
like bananas so much?
The have appeal.

How does a super hero
elephant ride to work?
In a trunk!

What sickness does Comet the
Super-Horse hate the most?
Hay fever.

What does Supergirl give Comet
to make him feel better?
Cough stirrup!

How did Superman stop the runaway elephant from charging?

He took away its credit card.

WHAT DO YOU CALL KILLER CROC IN A VEST?

An investigator.

BIZARRO'S OPPOSITE JOKES!

What do you get when you cross
Bizarro with a chameleon?
A chamele-off!

What do you get when you cross
Bizarro with a bison?
A bi-daughter.

Where do snakes in Metropolis get their news?
The Scaly Planet!

What do get when you cross
Superman's worst enemy with
a dinosaur?

Rex Luthor!

Why did Commissioner Gordon need
help arresting an octopus?

**Because it was
heavily armed.**

Why did Aqualad bring
fish to the party?
They taste good
with chips!

What do you get when you cross a
shrimp with Green Lantern?
Prawn Stewart!

What did Krypto the Super-Dog say when he sat on sandpaper?
Ruff!

I hear you went to an actual spider wedding?

Yes, and now they're newlywebs!

Why did Aquaman place the whales back in saltwater?

Because they didn't like pepper!

Why did Aquaman need help
capturing an octopus?
**Because the octopus
was well-armed.**

Why did Aquaman's seahorse,
Storm, cross the ocean?
**To get to the
other tide!**

Why does Aquaman command
seagulls to fly over the sea?
**If they flew over
the bay, they'd be
called bagels!**

What do you get when you cross a great white with Superman?
Shark Kent!

Why did Aqualad need an
umbrella under water?

**Because it was
raining catfish
and dogfish!**

How do Aquaman and Mera
communicate under the sea?

With shell-phones!

Why did Hawkman make a valentine
for Hawkgirl in art class?

**They were
tweet-hearts!**

Why did Cyborg buy a
great white shark?

**Because he wanted
more bytes.**

Which sea creature is almost as speedy as The Flash?
The Fastest Manta-live!

Which of Aquaman's ocean creatures
cries the most?

The humpback wail!

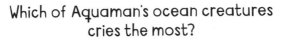

Why did Aquaman
order the elephants off
the beach?

**Their trunks
were too big!**

What do you get when
you cross an oyster with
a Kryptonian?

Super-pearl!

Where does Aquaman
listen to music?

At the orca-stra!

What is Aquaman's favorite
country to visit?

Fin-land!

Why are Aquaman's underwater
friends so smart?

**Because fish live
in schools.**

What's invisible and smells
like bananas?

Titano burps!

What do you get when Mr. Freeze forgets
to put on his pants?

A polar bare!

What kind of pet does
Mr. Freeze have?

Coldfish.

How did the Penguin know
it was raining cats and dogs?
**He stepped in
a poodle!**

Where does the Penguin
keep his money?
**In a snow
bank!**

What does the Penguin
wear on his head?
An ice cap.

Why don't alligators like to eat the Joker?

He tastes funny!

What's the difference between a fly and Superman?

Superman can fly, but a fly can't Superman!

Where did the
Super-Turtle get a new shell?
The hard-wear store!

CHAPTER THREE

Why did Superman go to
the school baseball game?

**He'd heard someone
had stolen a base.**

What did Cyborg tell the math student?

"You can count on me!"

Why did Metallo go to
the school nurse?

**He wasn't getting
enough iron.**

Why did Aquaman get an
A in music class?

**He was great at
conducting orca-stras.**

Why did Superman sit on
the school's roof?

He wanted to be
in high school!

Why did Krypto sleep under the bus at night? **He wanted to wake up oily for school!**

How do you stop Super-Dog from barking in the back of the bus? **Put him in the front of the bus.**

What did Superman say when he couldn't pass his algebra test? **"Clark can't!"**

Why does Clark Kent wear glasses in math class?

They improve his di-vision!

Why was Superman so good at subtraction?

He knows how to carry all those numerals!

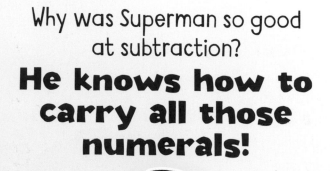

Why was Lois Lane so good at organizing her homework? **Because she'd daily plan it!**

What vegetable did Supergirl eat in the library? **Quiet peas!**

Why did Supergirl wear lipstick to history class? **They were having a make-up exam!**

Why did Cyborg spend all his time
in the cafeteria?

**He wanted
more bytes!**

Why did Cyborg pack fish for lunch?

**Because it goes good
with micro-chips!**

Why did Black Manta throw all the
library books into the ocean?

**He wanted to make
a title wave.**

Why did Wonder Woman study
in her Invisible Jet?

**She wanted a
higher education!**

Why did the teacher send Wonder Woman
home as soon as she arrived at school?
**Because she still had
her paj-Amazon!**

Where does Superman travel through time?

The cafeteria — because he always goes back for seconds.

Where does Doomsday sit in math class?

Anywhere he wants to!

Why did the Penguin get a penalty during basketball practice?

For fowl play.

Why did the teacher make Robin sit in the corner?

He said a bat word!

Why did Robin ask Batman
to join the school choir?

To perform a
Dynamic Duet!

What do you get when you cross a calculator with the Dark Knight?
A cal-crusader.

What is the Dark Knight's favorite thing he learned in school?
The alpha-bat!

What do you get when you cross the Dark Knight with a math teacher?
A bat-matician!

Why did young billionaire Bruce Wayne never get in trouble at school?

He always had the most cents.

Why did Robin bring a cake to school?
It was his bird-day!

What did Robin make in art class?
A bat-mobile.

What did the Joker shout when he jumped out of the janitor's closet?

"Supplies!"

Why was the Joker kicked off the baseball team?
He kept stealing second base.

What bird does the Penguin always bring to the cafeteria?
A swallow.

What happened when Harley Quinn joined theater class?

She stole the show!

What school subject does Poison Ivy like the best?

Geome-tree!

What is Poison Ivy's favorite grade level?
Kinder-garden.

Why is math Poison Ivy's least favorite subject?
Because she hates square roots.

Was Poison Ivy able to climb the rope in gym class?
Yes, she climbed up itch by itch!

Why won't Catwoman use a computer? **She's afraid she'll eat the mouse!**

What is Catwoman's favorite school subject? **Mew-sic.**

How is music class like Killer Croc?
They both have scales.

Why is Two-Face good at gymnastics?
He has a splits personality!

Why was the Penguin sent to the principal's office?
He was using fowl language!

What does
Mr. Freeze like best
about school?

**Snow
and tell!**

Why is Hawkman so good
in debate class?

**Because he has such
strong pinions about
everything.**

Why did Wonder Woman fly
her jet to music class?

**So she could reach
the high notes.**

What language class does
The Flash take?

Rushin'!

What is Elastic Lad's
after-school activity?
**He practices with
the rubber band!**

Did Bouncing Boy have a
good year at school?
It was up and down.

Why did Plastic Man wear
sunglasses to school?
**Because he was
so bright!**

How does Bumblebee get to school?
By school buzz!

Why did the Atom need a ladder
for school choir?
**To reach the
high notes!**

What happened when the Invisible Kid
lied about his report card?
**His parents could see
right through him.**

Why did Starro join the
debate team?
**He was good at
making points.**

How could you tell Martian Manhunter
didn't like the food in the cafeteria?
His face was green!

Why was Martian Manhunter
so good in Kinder-garden?
**He had a
green thumb!**

What school sport is Green Lantern the best at?

Boxing – all his power is in the ring!

What should you do if Green Lantern
forgets to set his alarm for school?
Give him a ring!

What is Hal Jordan's favorite schoolyard game?
Rings Around the Rosie.

What is Zatanna's favorite school subject? **Spell-ing.**

What did the art teacher get when she crossed Green Lantern with Aquaman? **Teal!**

Can Superman jump higher than a school building? **Of course he can, buildings can't jump!**

What do you get when you cross
Cyborg with a gym teacher?
A Cy-Ed Instructor!

Why does Beast Boy turn
into a dog at lunch?
"It's chow time!"

How does the teacher feel whenever
Superboy leaves the classroom?
She sees red.

Why did the math teacher sit in
Wonder Woman's Invisible Jet?
**She wanted her
lesson to be clear!**

What does Hawkman do when he forgets to study for a test?

He wings it!

Why did Bumblebee get sent the principal's office?

For chewing bumble-gum.

Why did the teacher give Hawkman an F on the test?

He was caught cheeping!

Why was Hawkwoman excited to go back to school?

She heard they built a new wing!

WHY DID THE FLASH SPEND SO MUCH TIME IN THE LIBRARY?

Because he was, well, red!

Why is Aquaman so smart?
Because fish spend a lot of time in schools.

How can you tell Aquaman
is smarter than Shazam?

**Because Aquaman
has three As and
Shazam only has two!**

How does Aqualad help
the music teacher?

**He knows how to
tuna piano!**

What do you call Jumpa's
school uniform?

A jump-suit.

Why did Starro quit teaching?

**He only had
one pupil!**

Why was it so hard for Aqualad
to get an A on the test?
**His grades were
always below C-level!**

What was the Penguin's
favorite meal in school?
Ice-burgers.

What did Aquaman use to build a
school building under the ocean?
SEA-ment.

What did the nurse give
Swamp Thing when he felt sick?
Plenty of room!

WHY DOESN'T THE FLASH EAT IN THE SCHOOL CAFETERIA?

He prefers fast food!

What's Titano's favorite
school sport?
Squash!

What do you get when you cross
a teacher with Gorilla Grodd?
**I don't know, but
you better behave
in its class!**

Why did Glomulus eat the exam paper?
**The teacher told him it
would be a piece of cake.**

What was Glomulus'
favorite number?
Ate!

What do you call a Bizarro backpack?
A frontpack.

What do you get when you cross
Bizarro with a teacher?
A teach-him!

Why did Bizarro bury
his math book?
**He wanted to grow
smarter!**

What did Cheetah say after lunch?
**"That sure hit
the spots!"**

When is Darkseid like a school supply?
When he's a ruler.

What kind of dog does Lex Luthor take to science class?
A lab!

During which school period does Lex Luthor put his robots together?
Assembly!

I DON'T FEEL WELL.

WHO WENT TO THE
SCHOOL NURSE'S OFFICE?

CLARK KENT – HE WASN'T FEELING SUPER!

CATWOMAN - SHE WAS FELINE BAD!

THE JOKER - HE FELT FUNNY ALL OVER!

BRUCE WAYNE – HE HAD A BAT COLD!

THE FLASH – HE WAS RUNNING A FEVER!

HAWKMAN – HE HAD THE FLEW!

MARTIAN MANHUNTER – HE WAS LOOKING GREEN!

AQUAMAN – HE HAD A SPLITTING HADDOCK!

THE ATOM – BUT HE ONLY HAD A LITTLE PAIN!

What after-school activity is
The Flash the best at?

Darts.

What happened when the Joker
stole a calendar off the
teacher's desk?

**He got
twelve months.**

Why did The Flash take a human
anatomy class?

**Because he's a
zoomin', of course!**

What does Krypto eat at snack time?
Pup-corn!

HOW DID THE FLASH FINISH HIS READING ASSIGNMENT SO QUICKLY?

He raced through all the chapters and dashed off a report!

Why did The Flash wear a helmet
in the school lunchroom?

He was on a
crash diet!

Why did The Flash go to the
school nurse's office?

He was feeling
run down!

Why did The Flash's classmates
in school like him so much?

**He was good at
making fast friends.**

What school supply does The Flash always carry with him?
An e-racer!

CHAPTER FOUR

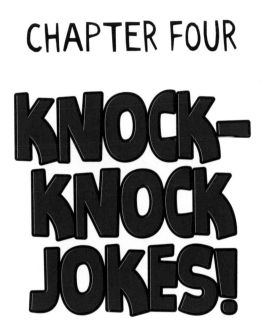

KNOCK-KNOCK JOKES!

Knock, knock!
Who's there?
Jet
Jet who?
Jet the back door, it's cold outside!

Knock, knock!
Who's there?
Wonder
Wonder who?
Wonder come out and play?

Knock, knock!
Who's there?
Diana.
Diana who?
Diana meet you! I'm your biggest fan!

Knock, knock!
Who's there?
Anita
Anita who?
Anita super hero to come help me!

Knock, knock!
Who's there?
Kanga!
Kanga who?
No, Kangaroo!

Knock, knock!

Who's there?

Perry

Perry who?

Perry-dice Island is where Wonder Woman comes from!

SUPERMAN!

Knock, knock!

Who's there?

Krypton

Krypton who?

Krypton side Superman's Fortress without being caught!

Knock, knock!
Who's there?
Mikey
Mikey who?
Mikey won't open the Fortress of Solitude?

Knock, knock!
Who's there?
Luke
Luke who?
Luke out! Here comes Superman!

Knock, knock!
Who's there?
Amos
Amos who?
Amos Supergirl fan!

Knock, knock!
Who's there?
Jimmy.
Jimmy who?
Jimmy some food. I'm starving!

Knock, knock!
Who's there?

Clark Kent.
Clark Kent who?

**Clark Kent come over to play
today, he's sick!**

Knock, knock!
Who's there?

Olive?
Olive who?

**Olive you, Superman!
(It's me, Lois.)**

Knock, knock!
Who's there?
Donut
Donut who?

Donut ask,
it's Bizarro!

Knock, knock!
Who's there?
Super.
Super who?
Soup or salad!

Knock, knock!
Who's there?
Lex.
Lex who?
Lex like my tooth is really looth!

Knock, knock!
Who's there?
Canoe!
Canoe who?
Canoe help us, Superman?

Knock, knock!
Who's there?
Iowa.
Iowa who?
Iowa lot to Superman for rescuing me!

Knock, knock!
Who's there?
Ivana
Ivana who?
Ivana fly like Superman!

Knock, knock!
Who's there?
Olsen?
Olsen who?
Olsen another sweep if you won't let the first one in!

Knock, knock!
Who's there?
Lois Lane
Lois Lane who?
Lois Lane down right now; she's tired from her adventure!

Knock, knock!
Who's there?
Luthor.
Luthor who?
Luthor than it was yesterday!

Knock, knock!
Who's there?
Cape.
Cape who?
**Cape put away your homework
and come outside, okay?**

Knock, knock!
Who's there?
Mister Wayne.
Mister Wayne who?
**Mister Wayne last night, cuz
everything's wet out here!**

Knock, knock!
Who's there?
Athena
Athena who?
Athena Bat-Signal in the sky!

Knock, knock!
Who's there?
Wayne
Wayne who?
Wayne the bathtub, I'm dwowning!

Knock, knock!

Who's there?

Police

Police who?

**Po-lice open the door!
It's the Gotham City police!**

Knock, knock!
Who's there?
Watson
Watson who?
**Watson side the Batcave?
I want to know!**

Knock, knock!
Who's there?
Kook
Kook who?
**Don't call me cuckoo!
The name's the Joker!**

Who's there?
Ken.
Ken who?
**Ken I come in? The Joker's
on the loose!**

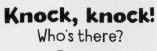

Knock, knock!
Who's there?
Alex.
Alex who?

Alex plain on the way to the Batcave, Robin!

Knock, knock!
Who's there?
Sparrow
Sparrow who?
Sparrow me all the questions, this is Robin, Boy Wonder!

Knock, knock!
Who's there?
Wanda
Wanda who?
Wanda go hang out with Robin?

Knock, knock!
Who's there?
Justin
Justin who?
Justin the Batcave for the very first time!

Knock, knock!
Who's there?
Raven
Raven who?
Raven lunatic, the Penguin! Quack, quack!

Knock, knock!
Who's there?
Tank.
Tank who?
Tank who for saving me, Batman!

Knock, knock!
Who's there?
Doris
Doris who?
Doris locked, so Batman will break it down!

Knock, knock!
Who's there?
Wayne.
Wayne who?
Wayne drops keep falling on my head!

Knock, knock!
Who's there?
Bruce.
Bruce who?
Bruce some coffee for us, I'm coming in!

Knock, knock!
Who's there?
Bat.
Bat who?
Bat you'll never guess!

Knock, knock!
Who's there?
Lantern
Lantern who?

Lantern down
on the runway!

Knock, knock!
Who's there?
Tess
Tess who?
Tess out this new aircraft, Hal Jordan!

Knock, knock!
Who's there?
Gus
Gus who?
Gus he has a cool power ring, that's why!

THE FLASH!

Knock, knock!
Who's there?
Kenny
Kenny who?
Kenny outrun The Flash?

Knock, knock!
Who's there?
The Flash
The Flash who?
The Flash doesn't have a last name. It's just The Flash!

Knock, knock!
Who's there?
Barry.
Barry who?
Barry the treasure where no one will find it!

AQUAMAN!

Knock, knock!
Who's there?
Howard
Howard who?
Howard you like to go swimming with Aquaman?

Knock, knock!
Who's there?
Philip
Philip who?
Philip this glass because Aqualad is thirsty!

Knock, knock!

Who's there?

Manta

Manta who?

What's the Manta with you?

AND
MORE!

Knock knock.
Who's there?
Interrupting Hawkman.
Interrupting Haw—
SKRREEEEE!

Knock knock.
Who's there?
Interrupting Joker.
Interrupting Jok—
HAHAHAHA!

Knock, knock!
Who's there?
Bumblebee
Bumblebee who?
**Bumblebee nice and open
the door!**

Knock, knock!
Who's there?
Hawk
Hawk who?
**Hawk come you won't
open the door?**

Knock, knock!
Who's there?
Martian
Martian who?

Martian in the super hero parade!

Knock, knock!

Who's there?

Atom

Atom who?

Atom all up, this is the tenth time I've knocked!

Knock, knock!

Who's there?

Ben

Ben who?

Ben down and pick me up, it's the Atom!

Knock, knock!
Who's there?
Hitch
Hitch who?
Hitch sure did explode!

HOW TO TELL JOKES!

1. KNOW the joke.

Make sure you remember the whole joke before you tell it. This sounds like a no-brainer, but most of us have known someone who says, "Oh, this is so funny . . ." Then, when they tell the joke, they can't remember the end. And that's the whole point of a joke – its punch line.

2. SPEAK CLEARLY.

Don't mumble; don't speak too fast or too slow. Just speak like you normally do. You don't have to use a different voice or accent or sound like someone else.

3. LOOK at your audience.

Good eye contact with your listeners will grab their attention.

4. DON'T WORRY about gestures or how to stand or sit when you tell your joke. Remember, telling a joke is basically talking.

5. DON'T LAUGH at your own joke.

Some comedians break up while they're acting in a sketch or telling a story, but the best rule to follow is not to laugh. If you start to laugh, you might lose the rhythm of your joke or keep yourself from telling the joke clearly. Let your audience laugh. That's their job. Your job is to be the funny one.

6. THE PUNCH LINE is the most important part of the joke.

It's the climax, the payoff, the main event. A good joke can sound even better if you pause for just a second or two before you deliver the punch line. That tiny pause will make your audience mentally sit up and hold their breath, eager to hear what's coming next.

7. The SETUP is the second most important part of a joke.

That's basically everything you say before you get to the punch line. And that's why you need to be as clear as you can (see #2) so that when you finally reach the punch line, it makes sense!

8. YOU CAN GET FUNNIER.

It's easy. Watch other comedians. Listen to other people tell a joke or story. Check out a good comedy show or film. You can pick up some skills simply by seeing how others get their comedy across. You will absorb it! And soon it will come naturally.

9. Last, but not least, telling a joke is all about TIMING.

That means not only getting the biggest impact for your joke, waiting for the right time, giving that extra pause before the punch line — but it also means knowing when NOT to tell a joke. When you're among friends, you can tell when they'd like to hear something funny. But in an unfamiliar setting, get a "sense of the room" first. Are people having a good time? Or is it a more serious event? A joke has the most funny power when it's told in the right setting.

MICHAEL DAHL

Michael Dahl is the prolific author of the bestselling *Goodnight, Baseball* picture book and more than 200 other books for children and young adults. He has won the AEP Distinguished Achievement Award three times for his nonfiction, a Teacher's Choice award from Learning magazine, and a Seal of Excellence from the Creative Child Awards. And he has won awards for his board books for the earliest learners, *Duck Goes Potty* and *Bear Says "Thank You!"* Dahl has written and edited numerous graphic novels for younger readers, authored the Library of Doom adventure series, the Dragonblood books, Trollhunters, and the Hocus Pocus Hotel mystery/comedy series. Dahl has spoken at schools, libraries, and conferences across the US and the UK, including ALA, AASL, IRA, and Renaissance Learning. He currently lives in Minneapolis, Minnesota, in a haunted house.

DONALD LEMKE

Donald Lemke works as a children's book editor. He has written dozens of all-age comics and children's books for Capstone, HarperCollins, Running Press, and more. Donald lives in St. Paul, Minnesota, with his brilliant wife, Amy, two toddling toddlers, and a not-so-golden retriever named Paulie.